Winning Recipes

A Collection of Delicious, Easy Dish
Ideas from Wales!

Table of Contents

Introduction

What makes Welsh food a wonderful trip into the food of the British Isles?

They love their food in Wales, as well they should. They have some of the finest produce you can find anywhere. Their landscape reflects the variety, freshness and quality of local foods. There are meats from local farms, veggies that have just been dug and fish that is fresh from their coastline.

Wales offers not only traditional recipes, but modern ones, as well. Their lamb is a feast to behold and can be prepared in several ways. The Welsh people enjoy and love sharing their traditional dishes too, like Welsh cakes, which are scones cooked on griddles. Their Bara Brith (speckled dessert bread) is a traditional treat that is still made often today.

You may enjoy the unique taste of laverbread. It's not actually bread – it's seaweed! It is fried into patties and served with eggs, fresh cockles and bacon.

In Welsh kitchens, they don't simply serve lamb. There is actually a considerable variety of dishes, especially considering the size of the British Isles. Whether you enjoy making traditional or modern dishes, there is something for everyone to try their hand at when it comes to cooking Welsh-style.

The recipes in this helpful cookbook will give you an excellent taste (pun intended) of the cuisine of Wales and how to make authentic Welsh dishes for your family.

Welsh Breakfast Recipes...

1 – Welsh Breakfast Laver Cake

Laver cakes are almost always served with Welsh full breakfasts, but they are sometimes served as side dishes, along with roasted meats. This recipe is simple and easy.

Makes 4 Servings

Cooking + Prep Time: 15 minutes

Ingredients:

- 4 oz. of laverbread (seaweed, canned or fresh)
- 1 oz. of oatmeal, fine or medium
- 2 tsp. of bacon fat

Instructions:

1. Mix oatmeal and laverbread together in medium bowl. Divide mixture in 3/4" thick, 2" round patties.

2. Heat heavy fry pan on stovetop burner. Add fat to pan. Heat to med-high. Carefully slide patties in hot fat one or two at a time. Quickly fry for two or three minutes per side.

3. Carefully lift patties from the pan and lay on plate with paper towels so they can drain. Serve as one part of traditional Welsh breakfast or use as a roast meat side dish.

2 – Milk Pancakes

These are a little different than traditional pancakes. They make an interesting addition to a Welsh breakfast. The preparation is somewhat like that for biscuits, but they are served like any basic pancakes.

Makes 12-15 Pancakes

Cooking + Prep Time: 50 minutes

Ingredients:

- 1 cup of flour, all-purpose
- 2 tbsp. of sugar, granulated
- 2 tsp. of baking powder
- 1/2 tsp. of salt, kosher
- 1 cup of milk, whole
- 2 tbsp. of melted butter, unsalted
- 1 egg, large
- 1 tbsp. of oil, vegetable

Your favorite toppings, like pure maple syrup, butter, powdered sugar, honey, whipped cream, preserves, jams, chocolate syrup or berries

Instructions:

1. Preheat the oven to 390F. Locate a heat-proof platter or cookie sheet for laying pancakes on so they stay warm.

2. Whisk salt, baking powder, sugar and flour in small sized bowl. Set it aside.

3. Whisk egg, milk and butter together in medium sized bowl. Add the dry ingredients into the milk mixture and whisk till barely moistened.

4. Place large sized frying pan on med. heat. Brush thin oil film lightly over pan surface.

5. Spoon a large tbsp. of the pancake batter into pan for each single pancake. Allow room so they can spread out a bit.

6. Cook till pancakes' surface have bubbles, some having burst. Carefully flip them with spatula. Cooked till underside has browned. Transfer to platter or baking sheet and loosely cover with foil. Keep them warm in the oven.

7. Continue with remainder of pancakes. Serve warm and add your favorite toppings.

3 – Cockles, Laverbread and Welsh Bacon

This is considered a full Welsh Breakfast, and it's similar in some ways to those served in other parts of the UK. The cockles and laverbread make it unique, though. You won't find them in Northern Irish, English or Scottish breakfasts.

Makes 4 Servings

Cooking + Prep Time: 50 minutes

Ingredients:

- 8 ounces of laverbread, prepared, canned, available online
- 2 ounces of oatmeal
- Pepper, WHITE, as desired
- 8 ounces of cooked cockle meat
- 1 ounce of butter, unsalted
- 1 chopped leek
- 2 ounces of fat, bacon
- 8 fried bacon rashers, smoked, crisp, for serving

Instructions:

1. Mix oatmeal and laverbread in bowl till combined well. Season as desired. Set it aside for 15-20 minutes.

2. Melt butter in fry pan till it foams. Add leek. Fry for three or four minutes, till they have softened. Add cockle meat. Cook for a couple more minutes, till heated completely through.

3. Dampen your hands. Pinch off some pieces of laverbread mixture. Roll into balls about the same size as golf balls. Flatten balls a bit, creating small patties.

4. Heat fat on med. heat in a separate pan. Fry laverbread patties a few at a time, for two or three minutes on both sides. They should turn golden brown.

5. Divide patties among four individual plates. Spoon over with leeks and cockles. Top servings with two rashers each of bacon. Serve.

4 – Extra Creamy Scrambled Egg Breakfast

This recipe is a spin-off of the typical full Welsh breakfast. You still have the cockles, and the laverbread made with seaweed. It's a popular meal especially in the southwestern part of Wales.

Makes 1 Serving

Cooking + Prep Time: 50 minutes

Ingredients:

- 1 tbsp. of laverbread

- 1 tbsp. of cockles, cooked
- 2 eggs, large
- Salt, coarse
- Pepper, black, ground
- 1 tbsp. of butter, Welsh
- 1 tbsp. of double cream, Welsh

Optional: toast

Instructions:

1. Melt butter on med. heat in small sauce pan.

2. Drain, then rinse cockles well and pat them dry with paper towels.

3. Beat eggs and 1 tbsp. filtered water in small bowl. Season it with coarse salt and ground pepper.

4. Pour the mixture into the sauce pan. Scrape the bottom frequently until mixture has barely set.

5. Stir in cockles, laverbread and cream. Heat till warmed through, but don't overcook the eggs.

6. Transfer meal to plate. Serve it with toast, as desired.

5 – Swansea Breakfast

You can serve this recipe in the form of a light snack at any time of day, but it **Makes** a most delicious breakfast. The dish combines local Swansea seafood with the seaweed-based laverbread, preferred in Welsh breakfasts.

Makes 4 Servings

Cooking + Prep Time: 25 minutes

Ingredients:

- 1 chopped onion, large
- 1 tbsp. of oil, vegetable
- 4 chopped bacon slices
- 3 & 1/2 oz. of cockles, cooked
- 4 & 1/4 oz. of laverbread
- Pepper, black
- Lemon juice, fresh

Instructions:

1. Heat large sized fry pan. Add oil. Cook onion for three to four minutes.

2. Add bacon. Cook till crisp.

3. Add cockles. Mix in laverbread. Heat well. Season with pepper and lemon juice and serve.

Welsh Recipes for Lunches, Dinners, Side Dishes and Appetizers

6 – Welsh Rarebit

You've probably heard of this Welsh dish before. This is a basic recipe, and it's a more contemporary reboot on the original toasted sandwich. Various ingredients can be added, like tomatoes, bacon, ham, leeks and herbs.

Makes 6 Servings

Cooking + Prep Time: 35 minutes

Ingredients:

For rarebit

- 1 oz. of butter, unsalted

- 12 oz. of cheese
- 4 fl. oz. of milk
- 1/2 tsp. of mustard, mild
- Salt, kosher
- Pepper, black, ground

For sandwich

- 18 bread circles, medium sized
- 6 thinly sliced, large tomatoes, ripe
- Parsley, flat leaf
- Salt, kosher
- Pepper, black, ground

Instructions:

1. To prepare rarebit, melt butter in pan. Add grated cheese. Stir on low heat till melted and pour in milk.

2. Add mustard and other flavorings you like. Season as desired. Bring mixture to close to the boiling point and remove from heat.

3. To create sandwich, toast or fry bread. Assemble 3-tiered sandwich with herbs, seasoning and sliced tomatoes between layers.

4. Place on baking sheet. Pour rarebit mixture over sandwich. Brown in hot oven at highest setting. Serve promptly.

7 – Merthyr Pie

This delectable dish tops tasty slow-cooked beef shin meat with a cheesy type of bread that is then fried in goose fat. It doesn't SOUND super, but it tastes great!

Makes 6 Servings

Cooking + Prep Time: 5 hours & 45 minutes

Ingredients:

For layers of beef

- 2 & 1/4 lb. of off-bone beef shin
- 2 halved carrots, medium
- 1 quartered onion, medium
- 2 halved sticks of celery
- 1 halved garlic bulb, small
- 3 bay leaves, fresh
- 1 sprig of thyme, fresh

For cheese and bread layers

- 5 & 1/3 oz. of beef drippings
- 8 sourdough slices, thick
- 3 to 4 tbsp. of mustard, English or Dijon
- 5 & 1/3 oz. of grated cheddar cheese

Instructions:

1. Heat oven to 285F.

2. Place beef shin in covered baking dish with herbs and vegetables. Pour water over, till it comes 3/4 up side of dish.

3. Cut baking paper piece so it sits snugly atop liquid and beef. Place lid on dish.

4. Place in oven. Cook for five hours, till meat is tender enough to fall apart when you test it using a fork.

5. Remove vegetables and beef from liquid and set aside so they can cool.

6. Bubble liquid in pot till reduced by 1/3. Reserve liquid.

7. Heat 1/3 of beef drippings in large sized fry pan.

8. Fry several bread slices for a few minutes on each side, till golden, but not yet fried completely through. Repeat this step with the rest of bread and drippings.

9. Spread fried bread with mustard. Flake beef shin roughly. Chop cooked veggies. Squeeze garlic from its skin. Raise temperature of oven to 350F.

10. To construct pie, place 1/3 of fried bread in dish bottom. Sprinkle with 1/3 of cheese. Add half of garlic, beef and chopped veggies.

11. Season as desired. Repeat process. Finish with last bread and cheese layer.

12. Pour 6 & 3/4 to 8 & 1/2 fluid ounces of reserved stock, wetting the bread but not drowning it.

13. Bake for 12 to 15 minutes, till cheese bubbles. Allow to sit for five to six minutes and serve.

8 – Baked Trout and Bacon

This is a traditional recipe that works fine with brown or rainbow trout. The most traditional dishes use brown trout, harvested from local coasts. When you wrap that trout in the bacon, it helps the fish to retain its flavor and moisture.

Makes 4 Servings

Cooking + Prep Time: 35 minutes

Ingredients:

- 4 rainbow or brown trout, whole
- 8 rashers of bacon, streaky
- 4 lemon slices

- Salt, sea
- Pepper, black, ground
- 1 handful parsley sprigs

Instructions:

1. Preheat oven to 350F

2. Wash, then dry trout inside & out. Season inside of trout with sea salt and ground pepper and several sprigs of parsley.

3. Wrap each trout with 2 bacon rashers in spiral shape around fish. Secure with cocktail sticks.

4. Lay trout side by side in shallow oven-proof dish.

5. Bake for 18-20 minutes till fish is flaky and cooked. Transfer to plates and serve.

9 – Spring Onion and Lettuce Risotto

This easy risotto recipe highlights some of the best fresh vegetables found during the spring time. Spring onions are sweet, tender and juicy, unlike many you find at the grocery store during other seasons. These onions make this dish special.

Makes 4 Servings

Cooking + Prep Time: 50 minutes

Ingredients:

- 10 trimmed spring onions
- 34 fluid ounces of vegetable stock, light

- 2 & 3/4 oz. of butter, unsalted
- 8 ounces of risotto rice
- 1 & 3/4 fluid ounces of wine, white
- 1 soft round lettuce head
- 1 small gem lettuce
- 1/2 lemon, grated zest only
- 1 & 3/4 oz. of grated Parmesan
- 3 & 1/2 oz. of crumbled goat cheese, creamy

Instructions:

1. Slice onions thinly. Separate green part from white. Bring stock to a boil in large pan. Keep it hot on low heat.

2. Melt 2 & 1/3 oz. of butter in medium pan. Add white part of onions. Gently cook for a minute.

3. Add rice to pan. Stir till all grains have been coated with butter. Gently fry for a minute.

4. Add white wine. Simmer till rice absorbs it. Add large ladle full of heated stock. Stir while simmering till absorbed. Add another ladle and repeat.

5. Continue with this process while continually stirring till rice has become creamy.

6. Cut all lettuce into strips of 1/2-inch width.

7. After 18-20 minutes, add lemon zest, parmesan and the rest of the butter. Continue cooking. Stir in goat cheese and green onion tops, then last amount of stock.

8. Cook for a few minutes longer, then add shredded lettuce and stir it in. Cook for a couple minutes till lettuce is barely wilting. Season as desired. Serve.

10 – Welsh Giant Oggie

This is a Cornish pastry, loved all through Great Britain. It is a part of their culinary heritage, and this is the Welsh version of the dish. These Oggies are giant pockets of food wrapped in pastry.

Makes 2 Servings

Cooking + Prep Time: 1 hour & 20 minutes

Ingredients:

For pastry

- 6 oz. of flour, all-purpose

- 1 pinch of salt, sea
- 2 oz. of butter, unsalted
- 2 oz. of lard
- 2-3 tbsp. of cold water, filtered

For filling

- 1 oz. of butter, unsalted
- 1/2 cup of sliced leeks
- 6 oz. of chunk-cut potatoes
- 6 oz. of cubed lamb
- Salt, kosher, as desired
- Pepper, black, ground, as desired
- 1 lightly beaten egg, large

Instructions:

1. Preheat the oven to 425F.

2. Place salt, lard, butter and flour into food processor. Pulse till mixture looks like bread crumbs. Slowly add water through a funnel till dough forms a ball. Wrap it in plastic wrap. Rest pastry for 1/2 hour.

3. Melt butter in sauce pan. Add leeks. Cook for five minutes over low heat.

4. Add potatoes to pan. Cook for five minutes more.

5. Add lamb pieces. Brown on all sides. Cook for a couple minutes, then cover and cook on low heat for five to six minutes.

6. Season pan contents with kosher salt and ground pepper. Set aside to allow for cooling.

7. Divide pastry in halves. Roll both pieces into rounds of about 8 & 2/3 inches. Brush rounds with the beaten egg.

8. Divide meat mixture into all pastry circles. Place on one side of circles. Brush edges with beaten egg.

9. Fold circles in 1/2 over filling. The two edges should meet. Crimp edges together and seal them. Brush them with last of beaten egg.

10. Place pastries on lightly greased cookie sheet. Bake for 12-15 minutes. Lower heat to 350F. Cook for 1/2 hour more till Oggies are golden brown. Serve while hot or allow to cool and serve.

11 – Lamb with Cheese and Olives

Lamb is used often in Welsh cooking, and there are many ways it can be prepared. In this recipe, you'll find the lamb to be hearty and succulent. It is enriched with creamy Welsh cheese and piquant tomatoes.

Makes 4 Servings

Cooking + Prep Time: 40 minutes + 20 minutes minimum marinating time

Ingredients:

- 4 slightly flattened leg steaks, lamb
- 2 tsp. of oregano, dried
- 2 sliced cloves of garlic
- 1 fresh lemon, zest only, grated
- 2 tbsp. of oil, olive
- 5 fluid ounces of wine, white
- 14 oz. can of plum tomatoes, peeled
- 2 & 3/4 oz. of pitted black olives, small
- 1 tbsp. of ketchup
- 3/4 oz. of chopped parsley, flatleaf
- 3 & 1/2 oz. of crumbled cheese

For serving:

- Green beans, cooked
- Mashed potatoes

Instructions:

1. Mix lamb with oil, lemon zest, garlic and oregano. Use ground pepper to season. Set lamb aside for 20 minutes or longer, to marinate.

2. Heat large sized fry pan on med-high. Brown steaks for a couple minutes per side. Add wine. Simmer for several minutes till it has been reduced by 1/2.

3. Add tomatoes to pan. Break them up a bit. Add ketchup and olives. Cook for 12-15 minutes, till lamb is done cooking.

4. Remove lamb from pan. Set aside on plate and keep it warm. Allow bubbles to reduce sauce till it is slightly thickened.

5. Tip sauce over steaks. Sprinkle them with cheese and parsley. Serve alongside green beans and mashed potatoes, if desired.

12 – Lamb Shepherd's Pie

The lamb in this dish is slow roasted, and the taste is simply delightful. If you have any leftovers, you can reuse them in a hand-me-down dish of shepherd's pie. Either way, the taste is luscious.

Makes 6 Servings

Cooking + Prep Time: 1 hour & 10 minutes

Ingredients:

- 1 tbsp. of oil, olive

- 1 chopped onion, large
- 2 chopped carrots, medium
- 2 chopped stalks of celery
- 3 chopped cloves of garlic
- 1 tbsp. of thyme leaves, fresh
- 2 & 1/2 fluid ounces of wine, red
- 17 & 1/2 oz. of shredded lamb, slow roasted
- 3 & 1/3 fluid oz. of stock, chicken or lamb
- 2 tbsp. of Worcestershire sauce
- 3 tbsp. of ketchup
- 1 tbsp. of pureed tomatoes
- 1 & 3/4 lb. of cubed potatoes, floury (grown for baking and mashing)
- 3 tbsp. of butter, unsalted
- 2 egg yolks, large
- 3/4 oz. of parmesan cheese, grated, + more to sprinkle

Instructions:

1. Heat oven to 390F.

2. Heat oil in large size fry pan. Cook garlic, celery, carrots and onions gently for 9-12 minutes, till they become tender.

3. Add red wine and thyme. Simmer for a few minutes. Add lamb, along with stock, pureed tomatoes, Worcestershire sauce and ketchup. Season as desired. Gently simmer for 12-15 minutes, till mixture has been reduced.

4. Place potatoes in large pot with salted cold water. Bring to a boil. Simmer for 10-12 minutes, till they are tender. Drain the potatoes, then return them to pan. Mash till smooth. Beat in egg yolks and butter. Stir in parmesan.

5. Spread lamb and its mixed ingredients in 3 pint baking dish. Top with mash. Sprinkle with extra parmesan. Season as desired. Bake at 390F for 23-28 minutes, till the top is bubbling and golden. Serve hot.

13 – Mushroom, Chicken and Leek Pie

This chicken, leek and mushroom pie recipe is so easy, and you can use pre-made pastry for the crust, if you don't have a lot of time. Using chicken meat from the thighs and legs gives this dish a richer flavor.

Makes 4 Servings

Cooking + Prep Time: 1 & 3/4 hours

Ingredients:

For pastry

- 7 ounces of flour, all-purpose
- 1 pinch salt, kosher
- 4 ounces of cubed butter, unsalted
- 2-3 tbsp. of filtered water, cold
- 1 beaten egg for glazing

For filling

- 3 tbsp. of oil, olive
- 12 oz. of leg and thigh chicken meat, boneless, skinless
- 2 sliced leeks, medium
- 4 ounces of mushrooms, baby button
- 1 tbsp. of butter, unsalted
- 1 tbsp. of flour, all-purpose
- 18 fluid oz. of chicken stock, hot
- 1 tbsp. of chopped parsley, flat leaf
- 1/2 tsp. of thyme, fresh
- 1 dash each kosher salt & ground black pepper
- 1 egg, beaten, for glaze

Instructions:

1. Use package instructions to make the pastry.

2. Heat oil in large fry pan. Add chicken. Cook for 4-5 minutes and stir occasionally, till chicken has browned on all sides. Remove chicken with slotted spoon. Set aside.

3. Add leeks and mushrooms. Cook for a few minutes and stir occasionally till leeks have softened. Then remove mushrooms and leeks. Set aside with chicken.

4. Add butter to pan. Melt on med. heat. Add flour. Combine well and incorporate all flour into butter.

5. Whisk while adding chicken stock slowly. Continue to whisk till you have created a smooth gravy. Cook for several more minutes and stir occasionally.

6. Add mushrooms, chicken and leeks into gravy. Add thyme and parsley next. Season as desired. Cook for a couple more minutes and set aside to completely cool.

7. Grease a 1-pint baking dish generously. Roll pastry and line dish with it.

8. Re-roll remaining pastry to create lids that will fit 1-pint dish. Place pastry and dishes in fridge to set for 20 minutes or more.

9. Heat oven to 400F. Place cookie sheet on center rack.

10. Place filling into pint dish.

11. Dampen edges of pastry with beaten eggs with a pastry brush. Cover with the lid of pastry. Crimp and seal edges. Use beaten egg to brush the edges generously.

12. Cut small hole in middle of lid for steam escape. This will ensure that your pastry won't become soggy.

13. Set pie dish on heated cookie sheet in oven. Bake at 400F for 35-40 minutes. Filling should be bubbling and pastry colored a golden brown. Serve it while hot or allow to cool and serve cold.

14 – Welsh Farm Chicken

This dish features individual Cornish game hens or young chickens in a tasty vegetable sauce. It is served while hot, along with a wonderful sauce. It's delicious!

Makes 6 Servings

Cooking + Prep Time: 1 & 1/4 hours

Ingredients:

- 8 medium tomatoes, ripe
- 3 game hens, Cornish

- 1/4 cup of oil, olive

- 2 tbsp. of butter, unsalted

For Sauce

- 2 round-sliced zucchinis

- 1 chopped onion, small

- 6 sliced mushrooms, small

- 1 crushed garlic clove

- A pinch each of kosher salt and ground pepper, as desired

Instructions:

1. Fill large sized bowl with cold water and ice.

2. Bring large sized pot of salted, filtered water to boil. Add tomatoes. Leave pot uncovered and cook for a couple minutes, till skins have loosened. Drain in colander. Immerse in the ice water for a few minutes so that cooking process is halted. Drain. Then peel and quarter the potatoes.

3. Remove wing tips and feet from hens. Cut each into halves.

4. Heat oil in pan on med. heat and add the butter. Once butter starts to bubble, add the chicken. Flip once while frying for 12-15 minutes, till chicken is browned evenly.

5. Stir in kosher salt, ground pepper, garlic, mushrooms, onion, zucchinis and tomatoes with chicken. Cover the pan and lower the heat.

6. Simmer and baste chicken frequently with sauce, till it has no pink remaining in the middle. This usually takes 18-20 minutes. Instant-read thermometer should read about 165F. Remove to serving plates or bowls. Serve.

15 – Welsh Stuffed Leg of Lamb

Many traditional Welsh recipes start by simply roasting the lamb. In this dish, however, it is slow roasted, along with bacon, garlic and parsley. The sauce elevates this dish to a delightful finish.

Makes 6 Servings

Cooking + Prep Time: 2 hours & 10 minutes

Ingredients:

- 2 & 1/2 lbs. of half lamb leg, boneless
- 1 handful chopped parsley, flat leaf
- 3 sliced garlic cloves, large
- 2 & 1/2 oz. of cubed bacon or pancetta
- 3 tbsp. of oil, olive
- Salt, sea
- Pepper, black, ground
- 5 fluid oz. of high quality wine, red
- 3 & 1/2 oz. of veal stock (beef stock will work, too)
- 2 tsp. of small-cut butter pieces, cold

Instructions:

1. Heat oven to 350F.

2. Remove the string from leg of lamb. Open out joint with the skin side facing down. Slash thicker meat parts so joint lays flat on cutting board.

3. Sprinkle pancetta or bacon, parsley and garlic evenly on surface of lamb. Drizzle with oil. Season as desired. Roll joint up. Securely tie with some kitchen string.

4. Place joint in large size roasting pan. Cook for an hour if you like your meat rare, or an hour and 10-15 minutes if you prefer medium.

5. Wrap joint tightly in foal. Allow to set for 8-10 minutes.

6. Pour off fat from roasting pan. Place over med. heat on stove top burner. Pour in wine carefully. Scrape up any juices that stick on the pan bottom. Reduce to sticky glaze.

7. Add stock to roasting pan. Stir thoroughly. Reduce by one-half.

8. Strain through sieve into small size sauce pan. Add butter. Gently shake pan till all butter has been absorbed. Adjust seasoning as desired.

9. Slice lamb. Serve promptly with sauce and greens.

16 – Tomato Rarebit

Tomatoes add the unique flavor to this rarebit. Cheddar cheese adds to the palette of tastes. You can serve this on toast with tea for a very traditional Welsh snack or use it for a hot lunch on a cold day.

Makes 4 Servings

Cooking + Prep Time: 25 minutes

Ingredients:

- 2 chopped tomatoes, medium
- 1/4 tsp. of baking soda
- 2 tbsp. of butter, unsalted
- 2 tbsp. of flour, all-purpose
- 1 cup of heated milk, whole
- 5 oz. of grated cheddar cheese
- 2 eggs, large
- 1 tsp. of mustard, dry
- 1/4 tsp. of cayenne, or as desired
- Salt, sea
- 8 toasted bread slices

Instructions:

1. Mix baking soda and tomatoes together.

2. Melt butter in sauce pan. Add and stir flour. Cook for a couple minutes while stirring consistently.

3. Pour warm milk in slowly. Stir till the mixture is smooth and thick.

4. Add in tomato mixture, then cayenne, as desired, eggs, cheese and sea salt, as desired.

5. Cook on low heat and stir constantly, till cheese melts and mixture is blended and smooth. Spoon over toast. Serve it hot.

17 – Cider Baked Ham

This recipe for baked ham is traditionally Welsh, and originally was cooked with Welsh Cider. Since this cider is not often found elsewhere, you can use any dry cider, as long as it's not too sweet.

Makes 6-8 Servings

Cooking + Prep Time: 1 hour & 50 minutes

Ingredients:

- 4 & 1/4 lb. boned, rolled, string-tied piece of ham, plain, uncooked

- 3/4 quart of cider, Welsh or dry
- 1 small sized bundle of parsley, tied with bay leaves
- 12 peppercorns, black
- Salt, sea

Instructions:

1. Place ham in stock pan. Cover with cider plus water, till all meat is covered. Add peppercorns, parsley and bay leaves. Bring to boil, then lower heat and allow to simmer for 50-60 minutes.

2. Preheat oven to 425F.

3. Remove ham from its liquid (you can use the leftover liquid to make soup). Dry ham skin with clean towel.

4. Wrap meat using foil layer. Leave skin exposed. Use sharp knife to make a few diagonal slashes on skin. Rub skin with salt.

5. Place ham in casserole dish. Roast at 425F for 18-20 minutes, till skin is browned and crisp. Remove from oven. Allow to set for 12-15 minutes. Thinly slice. Serve.

18 – Fennel and Leek Soup

This is a hearty but simple soup, featuring the Autumn flavors of fennel and leeks. Its additional flavor and full-bodied taste comes from onions, potatoes and celery. It's easy to make, too.

Makes 8-10 Servings

Cooking + Prep Time: 1 & 1/4 hours

Ingredients:

- 2 tbsp. of oil, olive
- 3 cleaned, sliced leeks, large
- 4 sliced celery stalks, large

- 3 large peeled, halved onions, white
- 1 sliced fennel bulb, large
- 2 peeled, cubed baking potatoes, large
- 1 tbsp. of salt, kosher
- 1 & 1/2 tsp. of pepper, black, ground
- 8 cups of water, filtered
- 2 bouillon cubes, vegetable

Instructions:

1. In large sized sauce pan on med-low heat, add potatoes, fennel, onions, celery, leeks, oil, kosher salt and ground pepper. Stir while cooking till veggies start softening and onions become translucent.

2. Pour eight cups of filtered water on vegetables. Bring to boil and reduce heat. Add bouillon cubes. Simmer on low, and stir occasionally to help the cubes to dissolve, till potatoes are starting to thicken soup and veggies are tender. Serve.

19 – Leek and Cheese Soufflé

Soufflés are usually considered rather sophisticated, but this recipe is actually simple and easy to prepare. Soufflés may be made savory or sweet in flavor, and this is one of the favorites in Wales.

Makes 6 Servings

Cooking + Prep Time: 50 minutes

Ingredients:

- 4 oz. of butter, unsalted, plus extra to grease
- 1 cleaned, matchstick-cut leek, medium
- 2 oz. of flour, all-purpose
- 2 tsp. of mustard, Dijon
- 1/2 pint of milk, whole
- 3 oz. of grated cheese, Swiss
- 4 eggs, large, with white and yolk separated
- Sea salt, as desired
- Ground black pepper, as desired

Instructions:

1. Heat oven to 385F.

2. Melt butter gently in large sized sauce pan. Add leeks. Gently cook till they have softened. Don't let them brown.

3. Add mustard and flour to pan with leeks and stir.

4. Add milk slowly and stir well, creating a glossy, thick sauce. After the sauce has thickened, season as desired.

5. Add egg yolks. Beat well till incorporated fully.

6. Add cheese. Stir till it melts.

7. Beat egg whites in medium bowl till set firmly and stiff.

8. Add 2 tbsp. of egg whites into soufflé base. This will loosen up the mixture. Fold in the rest of the egg whites in two installments. Be gentle. Retain the volume of the dish.

9. Grease six ramekins lightly with butter. Spoon mixture into dishes gently. You can fill up to within 1/2-inch of top of ramekins.

10. Place ramekins on baking sheet. Cook at 385F for 12-15 minutes, till soufflés have risen and are golden.

11. Serve promptly with crusty bread and green salad.

20 – Potato and Cheese Rissoles

These tasty rissoles are traditionally served with fish and chips in the South of Wales. They are a true Welsh comfort food, and a treat whether served alone or with other dishes.

Makes 8-10 Servings

Cooking + Prep Time: 2 & 1/2 hours

Ingredients:

- 2 lbs. of peeled potatoes
- 1/4 cup of butter, unsalted
- 6 yolks from large eggs
- Salt, sea, as desired
- 10 & 1/2 oz. of cheddar cheese shreds
- 1/2 diced onion, large
- 2 whole eggs, large
- 1/4 cup of water, filtered
- 1 cup of flour, all-purpose, sifted, if needed
- 1 cup of breadcrumbs, soft, if needed
- To fry: 1 qt. of oil, vegetable

Instructions:

1. Place the potatoes in large sized pot. Cover with lightly salted, filtered water and bring them to boil.

2. Lower heat to med-low. Simmer till potatoes are tender. This usually takes 15-20 minutes. Then drain them and mash them in pot till there are no remaining lumps.

3. Put the pot on low heat. Stir in the butter and stir constantly while cooking, till butter is melted and potatoes are not moist anymore.

4. Spread the potatoes in bottom of wide bowl. Place in refrigerator for 1/2 hour or longer, till completely cooled.

5. Beat the egg yolks (6) into the cooled potatoes. Use salt as desired. Stir in diced onion and cheese.

6. Shape this mixture into balls that are roughly the same size as tennis balls. Arrange them in a casserole dish. Refrigerate till completely chilled. This will take an hour or longer.

7. Beat water and whole eggs in medium bowl. Spread the breadcrumbs and flour into two wide bowls.

8. Roll the potato balls in the flour to coat them. Shake balls to remove any excess. Dip balls into beaten egg and coat well.

9. Press balls into the breadcrumbs and coat well on each side.

10. Toss balls gently between your floured hands so unstuck breadcrumbs can just fall off. Place breaded potato balls on plate while you bread the rest. Don't stack them.

11. Heat oil in large sauce pan to 375F.

12. Deep-fry the balls in small batches in the oil till they are all a golden brown in color. Add additional oil. Return oil to 375F as needed. Drain the fried potato balls on paper-towel lined plate. Serve.

21 – Anglesey Eggs

These eggs are not as beautiful for display as some others may be, but the flavor **Makes** up for the lack of aesthetic beauty. The mashed potatoes create a soft bed on which rest the eggs and the creamy, thick cheese and leek sauce.

Makes 2 Servings

Cooking + Prep Time: 45 minutes

Ingredients:

- 1 oz. of butter, unsalted
- 2 washed, sliced leeks, large

- 1/2 quantity of potatoes, mashed
- 1 cup of milk, whole
- 1 tbsp. of flour, all-purpose
- 3 oz. of grated cheddar cheese
- 4 peeled, quartered eggs, hard-boiled
- 3 tbsp. of breadcrumbs
- Sea salt and ground black pepper, as desired

Instructions:

1. Preheat the oven to 400F.

2. Melt 1 ounce of unsalted butter in large sized fry pan. Add leeks. Season as desired. Cook on med. heat for five minutes, till leeks begin softening. Be sure you don't burn them.

3. Increase heat a bit. Add flour and stir. Cook for a couple minutes while continuously stirring. Continue to stir while you add milk slowly. Cook for a couple more minutes to create a creamy, thick sauce. Simmer over low heat for about five minutes. Add 1/2 of cheese. Stir and recheck seasoning.

4. Butter baking dish generously. You'll be putting in layers of potatoes and the sauce.

5. Add mashed potatoes to cover base of dish with a thick layer. Arrange egg quarters neatly. Pour leek sauce on top.

6. Mix in the rest of the cheese and the bread crumbs. Sprinkle sauce over it.

7. Bake at 400F for 15-20 minutes, till the mixture bubbles and the top crust turns a golden brown. Serve by itself or with meat.

22 – Winter Potato and Leek Soup

This recipe uses simple flavors to create a satisfying, hearty soup that everyone seems to love. Its great taste **Makes** it perfect for a light dinner, side dish or a lunch.

Makes 6 Servings

Cooking + Prep Time: 1 & 1/4 hours

Ingredients:

- 2 tbsp. of butter, unsalted, plus extra as needed
- 2 cleaned, chopped leeks
- 1/2 cup of onion, chopped

- 6 peeled, cubed potatoes
- 4 cups of broth, chicken
- 1 cup of 1/2 and 1/2
- Optional: 4 oz. of cheddar cheese shreds
- 1 tbsp. of parsley, chopped
- 1 tsp. of garlic powder
- Sea salt & black pepper, as desired

Instructions:

1. Melt the butter in pot on med. heat. Stir and cook onions and leeks till they become tender.

2. Stir broth and potatoes into the onion mixture. Simmer till the potatoes have become tender. This usually takes 20 to 25 minutes.

3. Next, pour the 1/2 and 1/2 in the soup. Continue simmering till soup has thickened slightly.

4. Stir in garlic powder, parsley, cheese, sea salt and ground pepper as desired and cook till cheese melts. Serve hot.

23 – Glamorgan Sausages

This is truly a Welsh classic recipe. It is sometimes called "poor man's sausage", since it actually contains no meat. You probably won't find Lancashire or Caerphilly cheese in many areas, but you can use a strong cheddar, instead.

Makes 16 Small Sausages

Cooking + Prep Time: 40 minutes

Ingredients:

- 8 oz. of bread crumbs, fresh
- 4 & 1/2 oz. of cheese, grated
- 3 eggs, medium

- A bit of milk, whole
- Sea salt
- Ground WHITE pepper
- 1/2 tsp. of mustard, dry
- 6 oz. of shredded, sautéed leeks
- 1 heaping tbsp. parsley, chopped, fresh

For the coating

- 3 & 1/2 oz. of bread crumbs, fresh
- 1 egg, medium
- 4 tbsp. of milk, whole
- To fry: oil, vegetable

Instructions:

1. Place bread crumbs, parsley, leeks, mustard, seasoning and cheese in medium bowl. Combine well by mixing.

2. Beat eggs together, then add them to mixture in step 1. Mix to form firm dough, adding a bit of milk if mixture gets dry.

3. Divide mixture into 16 balls. Shape them like small sausages.

4. Beat egg. Add milk to egg and place bread crumbs on plate. Season them lightly.

5. Roll each little sausage shape in egg mixture. Drain it a bit. Roll in bread crumbs. Repeat till you have coated all the little sausages. Chill in refrigerator for an hour or so.

6. Heat a heavy fry pan. Add a bit of oil. Add sausages several at one time. Cook on med-low till color is golden. Sausages should be fried gently. You don't want them on high heat or they will brown outside but not cook through. Serve.

24 – Leek and Curried Apple Soup

Curry, leeks and apples create a magical combination of flavors. The leeks have a mild, appealing taste, which accents the tartness of the apples and the aromatic curry. They blend wonderfully together into an inviting, creamy soup.

Makes 4 Servings

Cooking + Prep Time: 40 minutes

Ingredients:

- 1 tbsp. of margarine, unsalted
- 3/4 cup of potatoes, diced
- 3 chopped leeks
- 2 tsp. of curry powder
- 2 peeled, then cored and chopped apples, Granny Smith
- 3 cups of broth, vegetable
- Sea salt & black pepper, as desired
- 1/4 cup of yogurt, plain

Instructions:

1. Melt the butter in sauce pan on med. heat. Add and stir curry powder. Cook for about a minute.

2. Add apples, leeks and potatoes and stir. Cook for three to five minutes.

3. Add broth. Bring to boil. Cover pan and reduce heat. Simmer for 18-20 minutes.

4. Puree soup in food processor. Season as desired. Serve swirled with yogurt.

25 – Lamb Cawl

Here is another classic Welsh dish. It's very wholesome, too. Lamb was traditionally used only in areas where it was readily accessible. In other areas, cawl can still be made with seafood, bacon or mutton.

Makes 6 Servings

Cooking + Prep Time: 1 hour & 50 minutes

Ingredients:

- 6 lamb shanks, small
- 2 pints of water, filtered

- 8 ounces each of peeled, diced potatoes, turnips, onions, leeks and carrots
- Herbs, one bunch: parsley, rosemary, bay and thyme
- 1/2 small cabbage
- 2 tbsp. of oil, vegetable
- Salt, sea
- Pepper, black, ground

Instructions:

1. Heat oil in large sized pan. Season lamb. Add to pan with onion. Brown on all sides.

2. Pour water over lamb and add herbs. Bring to boil and reduce heat to simmer. Cover. Cook for 35-40 minutes.

3. Add all veggies but cabbage. Bring up to boil again. Then reduce to simmer. Cook for 40 minutes more.

4. Shred cabbage. Add to cawl. Cook for three to five minutes. Serve.

Welsh Desserts... SO Yummy...

26 – Mamgu Rice Pudding

A dessert tastes perhaps its best when it's also a comfort food. You can serve this rice pudding with vanilla ice cream, if you like, for an added sense of indulgence.

Makes 4-6 Servings

Cooking + Prep Time: 2 & 1/4 hours

Ingredients:

- 3 & 1/2 oz. of washed, rinsed pudding rice

- 2 pints of milk, whole
- 1 & 3/4 oz. of sugar, granulated
- 1 oz. of butter, unsalted
- 1 slit vanilla pod
- 1 pinch of vanilla salt, sea
- To grease: butter, unsalted

Instructions:

1. Preheat oven to 325F.

2. Butter a 1 & 1/4 oz. baking dish. Place rice in it.

3. Add butter, pod, vanilla, salt, sugar and milk.

4. Cover dish with aluminum foil. Bake for an hour and a half.

5. Remove foil. Leave dish uncovered and bake for 20-30 minutes more. It should be a golden brown in color. Serve.

27 – Welsh Pikelets

These traditional pikelets are fluffy and thick, and oh, so tasty. You can serve with your choice of whipped cream, jam or other toppings.

Makes 4 Servings

Cooking + Prep Time: 1/2 hour

Ingredients:

- 1 cup of flour, self-rising
- 1 tbsp. of sugar, granulated
- 1 egg, large
- 1 tbsp. of melted butter, unsalted
- 1/2 cup of milk, whole, more or less, as needed

Instructions:

1. Sift flour into medium sized bowl. Add sugar and stir.

2. Make an indentation in the middle of mixture. Add egg.

3. Use wooden spoon to stir while pouring milk in gradually until you've reached your preferred consistency. Thick pikelets require thicker batter. Add melted butter and stir it into the mixture. Beat till smooth.

4. Heat skillet on med. heat and coat it with non-stick spray.

5. Drop batter in large spoonful's onto skillet. They should spread to two inches across.

6. When you can see bubbles on surface, flip the pikelets. Cook till other side browns. Repeat with all pikelets. Serve.

28 – Welsh Cakes

These classic cakes are sometimes called bakestones in Wales, since they have been traditionally cooked using a bakestone, which is a thick cast-iron griddle. For the toppings, you could also use tropical fruit, mixed fruit or orange or lemon rind.

Makes various servings depending on size

Cooking + Prep Time: 40 minutes

Ingredients:

- 8 ounces of flour, all-purpose
- 4 ounces of butter, unsalted

- 3 ounces of sugar, granulated
- 2 ounces of currants
- 1/4 tsp. of spice mix
- 1/2 tsp. of baking powder
- 1 egg, large
- 1 pinch of salt, kosher
- 1 bit of milk for binding ingredients

Instructions:

1. Sift spice mix, baking powder and flour together in medium bowl. Cut butter. Rub it into flour.

2. Stir in fruit and sugar. Pour in egg. Mix, forming a dough. Use a bit of milk if mixture seems dry.

3. Roll out dough on floured work surface to biscuit thickness. Cut rounds with pastry cutter or rim of drinking glass.

4. Cook cakes on greased griddle till they are golden. Don't use too high a heat, or they will cook outside too fast, without cooking in the center.

5. When cooked, remove cakes. Sprinkle with sugar. Serve with unsalted butter.

29 – Bara Brith

This recipe varies a bit from the traditional Bara Brith, since it used to be made on yeasted bread. This is now a widely-served version, with a moist cake and dried fruits soaked in tea, overnight.

Makes 8-10 Servings

Cooking + Prep Time: 1 hour & 25 minutes

Ingredients:

- 14 oz. of fruit, mixed
- 10 fluid ounces of hot tea, strong
- 8 & 3/4 ounces of flour, self-rising

- 1 tsp. of spice mix
- 3 & 1/2 ounces of sugar, dark brown
- 1 beaten egg, large
- For glazing: honey, pure

Instructions:

1. Place dried fruit in medium bowl. Pour tea over the fruit. Mix in sugar. Dissolve well by stirring.

2. Allow to soak for six hours minimum, or overnight.

3. The next morning, sift spices and flour into soaked fruit. Tea does not need to be drained. Add and stir egg. Blend together well.

4. Preheat oven to 350F. Line 2-pound loaf pan with baking paper.

5. Pour mixture into loaf pan.

6. Bake for about an hour. Cake should rise and cook through. Allow to cool on rack. Store for two days before you eat. Serve in slices with unsalted butter. Drizzle with a bit of warmed honey, if you like.

30 – Chocolate Welsh Truffles

Welsh sea salt and whisky from Wales have grown in popularity in recent years. The version here combines both these ingredients in a wonderfully indulgent, satisfying dessert.

Makes 4 Servings

Cooking + Prep Time: 50 minutes + 2 hours setting time

Ingredients:

- 2 & 1/3 fluid ounce of milk, whole
- 4 & 1/2 oz. of chocolate, dark
- 10 fluid ounces of double cream liqueur, Welsh if available
- 1 tbsp. of whiskey, Welsh if available
- 1 pinch of salt, vanilla

Instructions:

1. Boil milk gently in small sized pan.

2. Grate chocolate into medium bowl. Pour into boiling milk. Combine well using a whisk till you have a thick, glossy, smooth sauce.

3. Add cream liqueur. Set aside and allow to cool.

4. Whip the cream lightly in medium cold bowl till you have soft peaks that fall back on themselves a bit. Don't whip for too long.

5. Fold in chocolate sauce slowly with whipped cream. Add pinch of the vanilla salt.

6. Spoon mixture into plastic bowl. Chill in refrigerator for 2-3 hours, so it has time to set.

7. Use spoon dipped in hot water to scoop balls of the truffle mixture. Serve as a dessert alone or use as garnish for other types of desserts like lemon tarts. Finish up with pinch of the vanilla salt and mint sprig.

Conclusion

This Welsh cookbook has shown you...

...How to use different ingredients to affect unique Welsh tastes in dishes both well-known and rare. Welsh cuisine is not well-known around the world, but you'll recognize some of the dish names.

How can you include these recipes in your home cooking?

You can...

- Make full Welsh breakfasts, which you may not have previously heard of. They are just as tasty as the ingredients sound.
- Learn to cook with Welsh meats like lamb. They add a wonderful taste to any type of dish in which they are used.
- Enjoy making the delectable seafood dishes of the British Isles, including fresh mussels and cockles. Fish is a mainstay in the region, and there are SO many ways to make it great.
- Make various types of pastries like truffles and Bara Brith that will tempt your family's sweet tooth.

Have fun experimenting! Enjoy the results!

Printed in Great Britain
by Amazon

16074381R00052